Car Mania

MUSCLE CARS

Ryan James

A Stingray Book

SEAHORSE PUBLISHING

Teaching Tips for Caregivers and Teachers:

This Hi-Lo book features high-interest subject matter that will appeal to all readers in intermediate and middle school grades. It may be enjoyed by students reading at or above grade level as well as by those who are looking for age-appropriate themes matched with a less challenging reading level. Hi-Lo books are ideal for ELL readers, too.

Each book appeals to a striving reader's age and maturity level. Opportunities are provided for students to read words they already know while encountering a limited number of new, high-interest vocabulary words. With these supports in place, students will read more fluently while increasing reading comprehension. Use the following suggestions to help students grow as readers.

- Encourage the student to read independently at home.
- Encourage the student to practice reading aloud.
- Encourage activities that require reading.
- Establish a regular reading time.
- Have the student write questions about what they read.

Teaching Tips for Teachers:

Before Reading

- Ask, "What do I know about this topic?"
- Ask, "What do I want to learn about this topic?"

During Reading

- Ask, "What is the author trying to teach me?"
- Ask, "How is this like something I already know?"

After Reading

- Discuss how the text features (headings, index, etc.) help with understanding the topic.
- Ask, "What interesting or fun fact did you learn?"

TABLE OF CONTENTS

WHAT IS A MUSCLE CAR?

Muscle cars are large, two-door sports cars with powerful engines that are made in the United States.

They are called muscle cars due to their high power. They are some of the fastest cars ever made by American **automakers**.

The most famous muscle cars were built in the 1960s and 1970s.

POWERFUL AND POPULAR

These cars got very popular because they were lightweight and had powerful V-8 engines.

Drivers liked the high power-to-weight **ratio** that made them incredibly fast.

Ford, Chrysler, and General Motors were the largest companies that first built these cars.

FUN FACTS

Police use muscle cars. Alabama was the first state to use muscle cars for their highway patrol.

THE FIRST MUSCLE CARS

Oldsmobile created the first muscle car, the Rocket 88, in 1949.

Chrysler's 1955 C-300 could reach speeds of up to 120 miles (193 kilometers) per hour.

In 1957, American Motors Corporation released the Rambler Rebel, which could go from 0 to 60 miles (0 to 96.5 kilometers) per hour in only 7.2 seconds.

THE GOLDEN AGE

The 1960s is considered the golden age of muscle cars.

It started with the 1964 Pontiac GTO created by John DeLorean, Bill Collins, and Russell Gee.

The 1969 Chevrolet Camaro ZL1 was created for race car driver Dick Harrell, who wanted a Camaro for drag racing.

FUN FACTS

The Ford Mustang is actually a pony car, not a muscle car. It has a smaller V-8 engine and a smaller body.

A 30-YEAR BREAK

In the 1970s, muscle cars lost their popularity. With road laws getting stricter and gasoline prices going up, the cars got more difficult and expensive to drive every year.

But in the 2000s, Chevrolet and Dodge released updated **models** of the Camaro, Charger, and Challenger. These cars looked very similar to their older models.

New versions of these cars are still popular today.

LEGENDARY ENGINES

Muscle cars are most famous for their large V-8 engines.

These powerful motors have eight **cylinders** arranged in the shape of a V.

The most popular engine model is the Hemi. Its name comes from a **combustion** chamber that has a **hemispherical** shape.

FUN FACTS

Muscle cars were manufactured in Australia by Holden, Ford Australia, and Chrysler Australia.

DRIVING DOMINANCE

Muscle cars have rear wheel drive.

A long **driveshaft** directs power from the engine to the back wheels.

Strong **torque** spins the back wheels and launches the car forward.

MUSCLE CARS IN ACTION

Muscle cars are very common in drag racing.

In drag racing, multiple cars race against each other at high speeds over a short distance.

When muscle cars became popular, Ford started making cars to be used exclusively for drag racing.

TOP MODELS

Chevrolet Camaro

First production year: 1966

Average price: $30,000

Top speed: 202 mph (325 kph)

Dodge Charger

First production year: 1966

Average price: $30,000

Top speed: 203 mph (327 kph)

Dodge Challenger

First production year: 1969

Average price: $32,000

Top speed: 203 mph (327 kph)

Ford Mustang

First production year: 1964

Average price: $30,000

Top speed: 186 mph (299 kph)

GLOSSARY

automakers (AW-toh-make-uhrz): companies that make cars and other moving vehicles

combustion (kuhm-BUS-chuhn): the process of igniting and burning; a car's engine burns gasoline to produce hot gases that move pistons

cylinders (SIL-uhn-durz): chambers in an engine that look like tubes; gasoline is burned and turned into power inside an engine's cylinders

driveshaft (DRIVE-shaft): a rotating rod that transmits power from a car's engine

hemispherical (HEM-i-sfeer-i-kuhl): in the shape of a half-circle

models (MAH-duhlz): types or designs of products; carmakers produce many car models

ratio (RAY-shee-oh): a comparison of two quantities or numbers using division, usually expressed as a fraction

torque (tork): a force that produces rotation or a twisting motion

INDEX

AFTER READING QUESTIONS

1. What are muscle cars?
2. What decade is considered the golden age of muscle cars?
3. What types of engines are found in muscle cars?
4. What type of racing is associated with muscle cars?
5. Name three American carmakers who have built muscle cars.

ABOUT THE AUTHOR

Ryan James lives in Western North Carolina with his dog Bailey. His favorite race to watch is the Daytona 500. His dream is to own a Lamborghini. When he's not writing books, you can find him backpacking through Pisgah Forest, North Carolina.

Written by: Ryan James
Design by: Kathy Walsh
Editor: Kim Thompson

Library of Congress PCN Data
Muscle Cars / Ryan James
Car Mania
ISBN 978-1-63897-472-7 (hard cover)
ISBN 978-1-63897-587-8 (paperback)
ISBN 978-1-63897-702-5 (EPUB)
ISBN 978-1-63897-817-6 (eBook)
Library of Congress Control Number: 2022933101

Printed in the United States of America.

Photographs/Shutterstock: Cover & Title Pg ©Meritt Thomas on Unsplash, ©VoodooDot, ©Urse Major, ©4045; Pg 3, 7, 8, 10, 12, 14, 16, 20, 22 ©Urse Major; Pg 7, 11, 15 ©Mooam; Pg 4 ©Johnnie Rik; Pg 6 ©Bruce Alan Bennett; Pg 7 ©artistmac @flickr; Pg 8 ©Gestalt Imagery; Pg 9 ©Alden Jewell @Flckr; Pg 10 ©Greg Gjerdingen @flickr; Pg 11 ©Tyler B on Unsplash; Pg 12 ©D-VISIONS; Pg 13 ©Steve Lagreca; Pg 14 ©@Wiki; Pg 15 ©myphotobank.com.au; Pg 16 ©Tanhu; Pg 17 ©Bruce Alan Bennett; Pg 18 ©YES Market Media, ©Bruce Alan Bennett, Pg 20 ©Lawrence Carmichael, ©Tony Hisgett @ Flckr; Pg 21 ©Art Konovalov, ©Kevin Tichenor

Seahorse Publishing Company
www.seahorsepub.com

Published in the United States
Seahorse Publishing
PO Box 771325
Coral Springs, FL 33077

SEAHORSE PUBLISHING